# Summary

This report explores the complementary ideas and practices that civil resistance and peacebuilding approaches present, each from different points along the conflict transformation spectrum. Both strategies oppose violence in all its forms, and seek to pursue just peace by peaceful means. However, they take different approaches to conflict transformation, both in their analyses of the primary causes of violence and how they respond to conflict. The report then describes how civil resistance and peacebuilding can work in tandem throughout the four stages of transformation of asymmetric conflicts. Concrete examples are provided to illustrate the respective functions of constructive conflict (through civil resistance) and conflict mitigation (through peacebuilding) in transitions from latent to overt conflict, from resistance to dialogue and negotiation, and from conflict settlement to sustainable peace. It highlights in particular:

- the crucial importance of civil resistance as a violence prevention/mitigation instrument and as a pre-negotiation strategy for oppressed groups, enabling them to wage necessary conflicts through nonviolent means, thereby putting pressure on incumbent elites to redistribute power equitably;
- the usefulness of peacebuilding's conflict mitigation methods to translate civil resistance gains into mutually acceptable negotiated outcomes and to reconcile polarized relationships in the wake of nonviolent struggles; and
- the need for sustained civil resistance in post-conflict or post-war societies in order to prevent and oppose autocratic backlashes, to resist anti-emancipatory, and 'neoliberal' tendencies within post-war peacebuilding operations, or to put pressure on all stakeholders to implement their commitments to progressive state reforms and social justice.

The conclusion highlights takeaways for researchers, nonviolent activists and educators, peacebuilding practitioners and international agencies seeking to support constructive, effective conflict transformation.

# About the author

Véronique Dudouet is senior researcher and program director at the Berghof Foundation (Berlin), where she manages collaborative research projects on non-state armed groups, negotiations, post-war governance and civil resistance. She conducts regular policy advice, peer-to-peer advice and training seminars for or with conflict and peacebuilding stakeholders. She also conducts consultancy research for various civil society organizations and international agencies, and serves as Academic Advisor of the International Center on Nonviolent Conflict (ICNC) in Washington. She holds an MA and PhD in Conflict Resolution from Bradford University (UK). She has authored numerous publications in the field of conflict transformation, including two books: *Post-war Security Transitions: Participatory Peacebuilding after Asymmetric Conflicts* (Routledge 2012), and *Civil Resistance and Conflict Transformation: Transitions from Armed to Nonviolent Struggle* (Routledge 2014).

*Acknowledgements: I would like to thank my research assistant, Matteo Dressler; the external reviewer, Lisa Schirch of the Alliance for Peacebuilding; ICNC staff; and Michael Beer of Nonviolence International for their help and contributions to this report.*

# Table of contents

Summary ................................................................................................................................ 2
Introduction: Civil resistance and peacebuilding strategies toward just and
   peaceful societies ............................................................................................................ 4
Civil resistance and peacebuilding along the conflict transformation spectrum .......... 8
   Main elements of convergence and divergence ............................................................ 8
   Civil resistance: A strategy to wage necessary conflicts through nonviolent means ..... 11
   Peacebuilding: A comprehensive toolbox of conflict mitigation strategies .................. 13
Complementary roles of civil resistance and peacebuilding during the four stages of
   conflict transformation .................................................................................................. 17
   Stage 1 (Latent conflict): Conscientization through nonviolent mobilization ............... 19
   Stage 2 (Overt conflict): Violence prevention through constructive confrontation ...... 20
   Stage 3 (Conflict settlement): From resistance to dialogue ........................................... 23
   Stage 4 (Sustainable peace): The twin roles of institutionalization and campaigning
   to promote and protect transformative peacebuilding ................................................. 27
Conclusion: Strategic contributions and takeaways for activists, practitioners, trainers,
   educators, and international actors ............................................................................... 32
Bibliography ........................................................................................................................ 36

# Tables and figures

Figure 1: Civil resistance and peacebuilding as sub-components of conflict transformation   9
Table 1: Similarities and differences between civil resistance and peacebuilding ............. 10
Figure 2: The progression of constructive conflict in unbalanced relationships
   (adapted from Curle 1971) ............................................................................................. 18
Table 2: Civil resistance and peacebuilding strategies and impacts during the four stages
of conflict transformation .................................................................................................. 31

# Case studies

Box 1: Key definitions ......................................................................................................... 5
Box 2: Conflict awakening in South Africa ........................................................................ 20
Box 3: Genocide prevention through nonviolent resistance in Timor Leste ..................... 22
Box 4: Women's advocacy for peace in Liberia ................................................................. 24
Box 5: People power and peace negotiations in Nepal ..................................................... 25
Box 6: Post-revolution transitions in Tunisia and Egypt .................................................... 27
Box 7: Onset of democracy in South Africa ...................................................................... 28
Box 8: Civil resistance to externally imposed peacebuilding in Kosovo ........................... 29
Box 9: Post-war mobilization for positive peace in Nepal ................................................. 30

# Introduction: Civil resistance and peacebuilding strategies toward just and peaceful societies

*"For a lynching, all you need is an angry mob; for dialogue, you need an organized society."* Adam Michnik, Polish former dissident, historian, public intellectual.

This quote points to the double roles of the pro-democracy struggle led by the Solidarity trade union in Poland during the 1980s. On the one hand, it led a successful civil resistance campaign through building parallel underground institutions and engaging in direct nonviolent actions against a repressive state. On the other hand, it engaged in dialogue with the diverse social forces to build and sustain a national movement while it also emphasized openness to negotiations with the communist regime, provided the latter recognized it as an equal partner. Eventually, the government and Solidarity sat down as equals for the 1989 Round Table Talks. The combined efforts of resistance and dialogue helped bring about successful democratization and a more just and nonviolent society.

Expanding on the notions and practice of civil resistance (waged through nonviolent actions) and peacebuilding (advanced, among others, through dialogue and negotiation), this report explores conflict situations where seeming power imbalances underlay relationships between different conflicting groups. It demonstrates how civil resistance and peacebuilding approaches can complement each other. They do so analytically—as useful conceptual frames for understanding conflict transformation—and practically—as intervention strategies that aim to transform conflicts toward more sustainable and just peace, in other words, "powering to peace."

This report rests on four basic assumptions:

- Although civil resistance and peacebuilding—both as practical strategies and fields of inquiry—share a common commitment to "social change and increased justice through peaceful means" (Lederach 1995: 15), they are rooted in distinct approaches to conflict transformation;
- In conflict-affected societies characterized by acute inter-group power asymmetries, stable and enduring peace needs both sets of strategies, if employed

in a coherent and complementary fashion;
- Few attempts have been made to compare and bring together civil resistance and peacebuilding in a more systematic way by mapping their multiple areas of convergence and actual or potential synergy; and
- These 'revolutionary' (civil resistance) and 'resolutionary' (peacebuilding) approaches to conflict transformation (Lederach 1995) have largely grown in mutual ignorance—developing their own distinct sets of activists and practitioners, theories and scholars, interpretative frames and ranges of techniques, research centers and education programs, organizations and forums, constituencies and institutional allies (Dudouet 2011).

Based on these observations, this report seeks to explore the conceptual and empirical nexus between civil resistance and peacebuilding approaches, and to present them as complementary ends of the conflict transformation spectrum.

In particular, this report addresses the following questions:

- What are the main features which distinguish civil resistance from peacebuilding strategies in the context of acute socio-political instability and power disparities among parties affected by or prosecuting a conflict?
- What are potential areas of complementarity between civil resistance and

---

### Box 1: Key definitions

**Civil resistance** is an extra-institutional conflict-waging strategy in which organized grassroots movements use various, strategically sequenced and planned out, nonviolent tactics such as strikes, boycotts, marches, demonstrations, noncooperation, self-organizing and constructive resistance to fight perceived injustice without the threat or use of violence.

**Peacebuilding** encompasses all local, state-based or international strategies used to mitigate imminent, ongoing and past violent conflicts, and promote lasting and sustainable peace. A primary emphasis is placed on bottom-up and top-down methods to promote dialogue and peaceful relationships between conflict parties as well as conflict-affected societies—such as dialogue, negotiation and mediation, and to (re-) build institutions and infrastructures for peace.

Both sets of practices and scholarly approaches belong to the broader field of **conflict transformation**, a generic, comprehensive term referring to actions and processes which seek to address the root causes of a particular conflict over the long term, in the pursuit of just peace by peaceful means. It aims to transform negative, destructive conflict into positive, constructive conflict and deals with structural, behavioral and attitudinal aspects of conflict.

peacebuilding and how did these seemingly different practices play out in examples from the field?
• What can nonviolent activists learn from peacebuilding practitioners, and vice versa, in order to bring about positive and sustainable social change?

*Civil resistance and peacebuilding both seek to address the root causes of a particular conflict over the long term, in the pursuit of just peace by peaceful means.*

If the normative goal of conflict transformation is to achieve positive peace by eliminating the behavioral, attitudinal and structural sources of violence (Galtung 1969, 1996), then a central feature of any conflict transformation strategy should be the pursuit of just and equitable relations in a conflict-affected society. A primary source of analytical inspiration for this report is Adam Curle's model which depicts the main conflict stages between powerful and powerless groups characterized by extreme asymmetric relations. This framework seems particularly suited to the exploration of the respective roles of civil resistance and peacebuilding during the various phases of conflict transformation processes (Curle 1971, Woodhouse and Lederach 2016) as it helps to highlight in particular:

• The crucial importance of civil resistance for violence prevention or mitigation, and as a pre-negotiation strategy that can be used by oppressed groups, enabling them to wage necessary conflicts through nonviolent means and thereby to put pressure on incumbent elites to redistribute power equitably;
• The usefulness of peacebuilding's conflict mitigation methods to translate civil resistance gains into mutually acceptable negotiated outcomes between the conflict protagonists and to reconcile polarized relationships in the wake of nonviolent struggles;
• The need for sustained civil resistance in post-conflict or post-war societies in order to prevent and oppose autocratic backlashes, to resist anti-emancipatory, and "neoliberal" tendencies within post-war peacebuilding operations, or to put pressure on all stakeholders to implement their commitments to progressive state reforms and social justice.

Next to Curle's model, the report also draws on other scholar-practitioners whose work lies at the interface between both fields of peacebuilding and civil resistance (such as

John-Paul Lederach and Dianna Francis), and on the author's own experience and past research (e.g., Dudouet 2005, 2011, 2013, 2014). In addition, the report refers to empirical examples from South Africa, Nepal, Kosovo, Timor Leste, Poland, Liberia and Tunisia where peacebuilding activities have preceded, accompanied or followed civil resistance campaigns and vice versa.

The section that follows will explore the areas of divergence and convergence of civil resistance and peacebuilding. The subsequent section will focus on the complementary roles of civil resistance and peacebuilding in the four main stages of conflict transformation as outlined in Curle's model. Finally, this report identifies concrete lessons learned for diverse audiences, namely:

- Conceptual implications and areas for further research;
- Practical recommendations for nonviolent grassroots activists, peacebuilding practitioners, and trainers and educators who support and promote civil resistance; and
- Policy lessons for international actors (bilateral donors, diplomats and inter-governmental agencies) seeking to identify, encourage, or support constructive and effective conflict transformation processes.

# Civil resistance and peacebuilding along the conflict transformation spectrum

Practitioner[1], educational[2] and scholarly worlds[3] have shown a growing interest in the interface between the "revolutionary" and "resolutionary" approaches to conflict transformation. Nevertheless, there is still little understanding within the peacebuilding community about the nature and role of civil resistance in addressing acute socio-political conflicts, and vice versa. Any attempt to map and compare civil resistance and peacebuilding should thus start by defining their analytical similarities, boundaries and distinctions, before outlining the practical areas of mutual complementarity and strategic synergy.

## *Main elements of convergence and divergence*

The main **similarities** between civil resistance and peacebuilding strategies are linked to the fact that they both ascribe to the conflict transformation paradigm, broadly defined around the pursuit of just peace by peaceful means. More precisely, conflict transformation approaches seek to address all core dimensions of violence in a comprehensive and holistic fashion:

- from direct/behavioral violence to "negative" peace through the restoration of the state's monopoly over the legitimate use of force;
- from cultural/attitudinal violence to transitional justice, reconciliation and forgiveness; and
- from structural violence to democracy, justice, equality and empowerment.

---

[1] For instance, the USIP seminar on 'nonviolent civil resistance and peacebuilding' (Rupert 2015), or the new working group on Nonviolent Movements and Conflict Transformation (NMCT) set up in 2016 by the Alliance for Peacebuilding network.
[2] In the United States, a few universities such as Notre Dame University, Eastern Mennonite University and American University have long-established teaching programs located at the intersection between nonviolence and peacebuilding.
[3] See especially the works of Lederach 1995, Weber 2001, Francis 2002, 2010, Schirch 2004, Clark 2005, Finengan and Hackley 2008, Kriesberg 2012, Vinthagen 2015, Stephan 2016, Wanis-St John and Rosen (forthcoming).

The concept of conflict transformation also draws a distinction between conflict and violence. While violence in all its forms should be prevented or eradicated, conflict can represent a positive force for change. In other words, destructive, violent forms of conflict ought to be transformed into constructive, peaceful ones (Wehr et al. 1996, Ramsbotham et al. 2011).

There also are some major areas of **divergence,** in terms of their ethical (impartial or value-based) orientation and diagnostic regarding the primary causes of conflict, the specific set of methods used to prosecute or mitigate conflict, and the primary locus and identity of change agents.

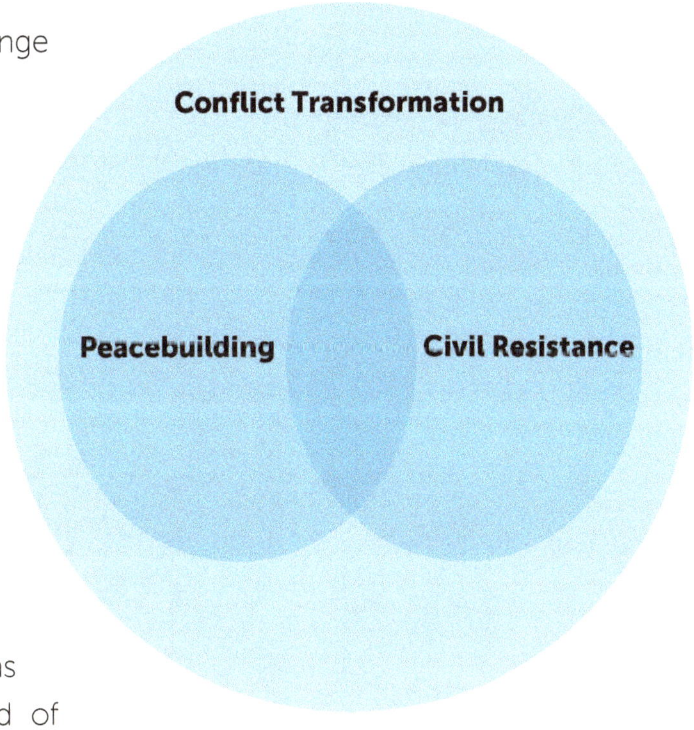

Peacebuilding theory and practice encompasses quite a diverse range of approaches, some of which are quite distinct from civil resistance, while others are conceptually, normatively or strategically aligned with the ethos and practice of nonviolent struggles. Figure 1 depicts these two approaches as sub-elements of the larger field of conflict transformation, which are partly overlapping, partly divergent.

**Figure 1: Civil resistance and peacebuilding as sub-components of conflict transformation**

Conflict Transformation

Peacebuilding | Civil Resistance

Table 1 below provides a more systematic comparison of the main areas of convergence and divergence between civil resistance and peacebuilding, both seen as conceptual approaches and practical strategies of conflict intervention.

## Table 1: Similarities and differences between civil resistance and peacebuilding

|  | Civil Resistance | Peacebuilding |
|---|---|---|
| **Means and ends** | General orientation: Just peace by peaceful means<br>a. Normative end goal: explicit value-bias in favor of positive (behavioral, attitudinal, structural) peace<br>b. (Principled or pragmatic) opposition to physical violence as a means of achieving social and political change | |
| **Ethical orientation toward conflict parties** | Pro-justice stance, ethical bias towards the empowerment of marginalized groups | Impartial or pro-stability stance |
| **Conflict intervention methods** | Contentious, extra-institutional methods of (nonviolent) conflict intensification (such as protest, civil disobedience or self-organizing) | Conventional methods of conflict mitigation (such as dialogue, negotiation, reconciliation, institution-building, structural reform) |
| **Agents of change** | Bottom-up approach: grassroots activists, institutional 'allies', third-party accompaniment and cross-border solidarity networks | Multi-track approach: international and national leaders, civil society and grassroots bridge-builders |

## Civil resistance: A strategy to wage necessary conflicts through nonviolent means

Although one can find accounts of civil resistance practice from as early as the Roman Empire (King 2007), it appeared as a more strategic and conscious method of collective political action during various independence and anti-colonial struggles of the 18th and the 19th centuries.[4] It was not until Mohandas Gandhi and his campaigns for civil rights and national liberation in South Africa (1906-1914) and India (1919-1948) that civil resistance was perfected as nonviolent practice and theoretical concept as a clear strategy that could be thoroughly planned and executed with a level of discipline equal only to that of a trained army. Gandhi's methods have subsequently been emulated and adapted to various national contexts. They have achieved worldwide success through the effective demonstration of "people power" on all continents and in countries with different political systems and cultures. In the past 15 years, nonviolent struggles have received global attention thanks to the so-called "color revolutions" in Southeast/Eastern Europe and Central Asia during the early/mid-2000s, followed by the "Arab revolutions" a decade later. In both sets of cases, massive street protests led to the resignation or overthrow of leaders considered by their opponents to be corrupt or authoritarian.[5]

As illustrated by these examples, and as defined by experts (e.g., Lakey 1987, Semelin 1993, Randle 1994, Schock 2005, Ackerman and DuVall 2000, Chenoweth and Stephan 2011), the term civil resistance denotes the use of contentious, extra-institutional, nonviolent collective methods such as strikes, demonstrations, boycotts, noncooperation and constructive resistance actions to challenge oppression, discrimination, external occupation, or any other forms of unjust social relations. The term "civil" in civil resistance refers to the "people power" of organized grassroots activists (as opposed to e.g., state elites or armed groups), who collectively employ legal, semi-legal or banned **bottom-up nonviolent methods** to pursue social change. It is especially appropriate for situations

---

[4] Examples of its use during the 19th century include a 10-year nonviolent resistance campaign led by the American colonists against the British that de facto liberated most of the colonies well before the war broke out; the Hungarian "passive resistance" against the Austrians that led to the establishment of the dual monarchy in 1867; or the Polish decades-long, nonviolent constructive resistance in the form of "organic work" that helped preserve and strengthen the national fabric of the partitioned nation (Bartkowski 2013).
[5] For recent findings on the rise of nonviolent movements and their effectiveness, see Chenoweth and Stephan 2016.

of power asymmetry between dominant (power-holders) and dominated groups.

In his seminal 1973 manual, Gene Sharp documented 198 different forms of nonviolent action, classified into three categories of methods according to their strategic function: nonviolent protest and persuasion, (social, economic or political) non-cooperation, and nonviolent intervention. The last category involves direct physical obstruction to change a given situation, either negatively (by disrupting normal or established social relations) or positively (through creative actions forging new autonomous social relations). Other typologies have been proposed, classifying civil resistance along methods of omission and commission (Sharp 1973), or methods of concentration and dispersion (Schock 2013).

In line with the conflict transformation paradigm, civil resistance strategies seek to address all three dimensions of violence (behavioral, attitudinal and structural) by:

- preventing individual and collective violent acts and redirecting them toward nonviolent methods of struggle;
- mitigating inter-group enmity and hatred by aiming to fight injustice rather than to destroy an opponent, and by pursuing constructive strategies to shift elite loyalties towards civil resisters;
- employing means and pursuing ends that embody democratic decision-making and equalize state-society relations.

A fundamental component of civil resistance is its **pro-justice and anti-status-quo orientation**. It is directed against oppression, domination and other forms of injustice maintained and supported by state authorities or any other political, social, economic or cultural elites (or "pillars of power"). Contemporary nonviolent action theory, pioneered by Sharp in the 1970s, is rooted in a thorough analysis of the dimensions of oppressive power by the "rulers" (Sharp 1973) that obstructs social justice—a situation that "gives all parties an equal opportunity to determine their future" (Chupp 1991: 3). Ordinary, seemingly powerless people can be powerful agents of change, even against materially stronger opponents. A large segment of civil resistance scholarship focuses on nonviolent struggles against dictatorship, but there are also comprehensive accounts of the use of civil resistance against other forms of injustice, such as national liberation struggles (Bartkowski 2013), contemporary decolonialization struggles (Chabot and Vinthagen 2015), land right movements (Schock 2015), campaigns against corruption (Beyerle 2014), and self-determination movements (Cunningham 2013).

In its approach to conflict intervention, civil resistance is described as a form of **extra-institutional contentious collective action**. It operates outside the bounds of conventional political channels (Schock 2005), by bypassing or violating the routine conflict resolution procedures of a political system (McAdam et al. 2001). In that sense, it can be described as a functional equivalent to armed resistance (Tarrow 2011: 7). The main difference between civil resistance and armed resistance lies in the use or absence of direct violence, which intentionally inflicts physical damage to persons or property (Bond et al. 1997).

## Peacebuilding: A comprehensive toolbox of conflict mitigation strategies

If, in its broadest interpretation, peacebuilding practice is as old as civil resistance, the usage of the term is quite recent. It was only popularized in 1992 when then-U.N. Secretary General Boutros Boutros-Ghali published "An Agenda for Peace." In his proposed typology of conflict intervention strategies, peacebuilding referred quite strictly to post-war recovery and reconstruction methods that aimed to strengthen peace and reduce chances for the relapse of violent conflict, primarily through U.N.-led operations. The term was coined to distinguish such methods from those of peacekeeping—international interventions under U.N. Chapter VII undertaken to separate belligerents in inter-state or intra-state wars—and "peacemaking," which involves third-party approaches to facilitate negotiations towards a peace agreement.[6]

Since the 1990s, the field of peacebuilding has expanded well beyond the narrowly defined understanding of peacebuilding initially proposed by the U.N. For many

---

[6] The distinction between peacekeeping, peacemaking and peacebuilding was first elaborated by Galtung (1976).

proponents of the concept of peacebuilding, it should be understood as encompassing not only internationally led forms of intervention, but also bottom-up and locally led approaches. Moreover, it should not only be restricted to post-war processes, but its methods are relevant during all phases of conflict transformation, including preventive diplomacy, peace processes, short-term post-war stabilization and recovery (e.g., disarmament, demobilization and reintegration [DDR]), and long-term post-conflict policies (e.g., security sector reform, transitional justice, reconciliation and democratic consolidation). In other words, peacebuilding efforts can be employed before, during, and after violent conflict occurs, by a wide range of actors in government and civil society, at the community, national, and international levels.

In line with the conflict transformation paradigm, peacebuilding strategies seek to address all three dimensions of violent conflict (behavioral, attitudinal and structural) by:

- negotiating ceasefires and comprehensive peace accords;
- redefining violent relationships into constructive and cooperative patterns through formal or informal dialogue and reconciliation efforts (Lederach 1997); and
- reforming oppressive state structures and policies, and building mechanisms and "infrastructures for peace" (Unger et al. 2013) that can address the root causes of conflict by providing platforms for their peaceful resolution through dialogue and collaborative decision-making.

In contrast to civil resistance, and despite their variety, all these peacebuilding strategies share a common focus on **methods to mitigate tension and adversity**: they seek to de-escalate the level of violent conflict, while civil resistance methods aim to intensify a conflict towards its necessary resolution.

While civil resistance methods are exclusively used by grassroots activists, the peacebuilding "toolbox" embodies **multi-track intervention** at different levels of a society. As widely popularized by Lederach's (1997) "pyramid," peacebuilders might belong to the top-level of decision-makers (Track I), the intermediate level of influential individuals such as civil society leaders or civil servants (Track II), or the grassroots level of community-based actors (Track III). On the one hand, international state and inter-state agencies have traditionally prioritized top-down "'state-building" interventions that focus on building the capacity of the formal state apparatus to strengthen the rule of law, guarantee human security, behave democratically or promote equitable access to resources—often dubbed "liberal" peacebuilding for their tendency to impose or promote external, Western agendas (Chandler 2010, Boege et al. 2009). On the other hand, local and international NGOs prioritize "peacebuilding from below" (Ramsbotham et al. 2011) by seeking to strengthen locally rooted approaches to inter-group dialogue, reconciliation or transitional justice. Their assumption or "theory of change" is that inclusive transition processes and bottom-up civil society empowerment are necessary preconditions for sustainable peace (e.g., Paffenholz 2010, Guardian 2015).

Whether located within conflict-ridden societies (as internal bridge-builders) or intervening from the outside (as mediators, facilitators, humanitarian agencies or international mission staff), all peacebuilders share a common self-identification as ***impartial third parties***. They do not belong to, nor associate themselves with, the primary conflict parties. However, such an impartial stance might be problematic in situations of acute conflict asymmetry between powerful elites and excluded minorities or disempowered majorities, where non-partisanship can be equated with indifference to oppression, and by extension, with the reinforcement of an unjust system (Lederach 1995, Francis 2002). Most peacebuilding organizations uphold a transformative agenda that recognizes economic injustice, and denial of rights and participation as underlying drivers of violence. Yet in practice, most international support programs tend to apply a technical approach to peacebuilding, which takes structural conditions as given. This approach also aims to implement technical reforms in a specific domain without necessarily challenging the engrained structural system of persistent injustice (Ficher and Zimina 2009). Domestic, locally led peacebuilding instruments such as national dialogues or traditional conflict resolution mechanisms have also been criticized for promoting the repressive status-quo ante or prioritizing stability at the expense of deeper socio-economic or political transformation (Youngs 2014, Boege 2011). This stands in contrast to the declared goals

> *Peacebuilding strategies seek to de-escalate the level of violent conflict, while civil resistance methods aim to intensify a conflict towards its necessary resolution.*

of peacebuilding approaches to tackle the structural conditions that foster conflict, such as social injustice, skewed land distribution or unequal political representation, among others (Ramsbotham et al. 2011).

Besides the outstanding works of a few scholar-practitioners such as Lederach (1995), Francis (2002), Schirch (2004), Fisher and Zimina (2009) and Kriesberg and Dayton (2012), **the role of civil resistance has been so far barely acknowledged within the peacebuilding literature**. Approaches that emphasize the need for "peacebuilding from below" tend to focus their attention primarily on professional NGOs, or on institutional channels for civil society organizations to voice their grievances and influence change, through monitoring, advocacy, facilitation or legal action (e.g., Reichler and Paffenholz 2000, Van Tongeren et al. 2010, Paffenholz 2010). For its part, the critical constructivist school has explored modes of local resistance to foreign-dominated liberal peacebuilding interventions (e.g., Richmond 2010, McGinty 2012). However, it mainly focuses on "hidden" and "everyday resistance" by individuals (Scott 1985) while neglecting the role of collective campaigns and constructive resistance actions by nonviolently mobilized and organized communities, groups and individuals.

Based on this cross-comparison of the analytical underpinnings and applications of civil resistance and peacebuilding, the next section presents the most important areas of complementarity between these two distinct approaches to conflict and violence. In particular, it highlights four main stages of conflict transformation processes when civil resistance methods might reinforce or contribute to peacebuilding, and vice versa.

# Complementary roles of civil resistance and peacebuilding during the four stages of conflict transformation

Acute socio-political conflicts can be described as transformative dialectic processes that move through certain phases, transforming relationships and social organization. This section will focus on the dynamics of asymmetric conflicts, which are rooted in structural power imbalance between contending societal groups, defined by "the extent to which one party to a relationship is able to dominate another" (Curle 1971: 6). In fact, most contemporary armed conflicts may be described as asymmetric, whereby a state (or occupying force) that is powerful in military, economic and political terms is challenged by insurgent groups often representing communities with seemingly much weaker powers. The government has legitimacy, sovereignty, domestic and international allies, armies, and access to resources. The insurgents have to fight for all of these (Zartman 1996: 8).

This section will describe civil resistance as a useful complement to peacebuilding strategies during the various stages of transformation of asymmetric conflicts. These stages are based on a diagram (see Figure 2) originally designed by the Quaker peace researcher/practitioner Adam Curle (1971), further developed by Lederach (1995) and Francis (2002), and recently re-popularized in a monograph retracing Curle's life and legacy as a "radical peacemaker" (Woodhouse and Lederach 2016). This diagram depicts the main stages and processes "which will usually need to be passed through if a situation of oppression ... with an extreme imbalance of power ... is to be transformed into one of genuine peace" (Francis 2002: 54). Four main transition stages and types of intervention are depicted:
   1. **latent conflict**
   2. **overt conflict**
   3. **conflict settlement**
   4. **sustainable peace**

These stages are characterized by:
   - different degrees of power imbalance between the conflict parties (from

unbalanced to balanced);
- different levels of situational awareness of these parties about their conflict-related interests and needs (from low to high); and
- different types of external environment (from a rigidity of status quo, instability of open warfare to the dynamic nature of peace and its consolidation).

Most conflicts do not develop in such a simplistic and linear fashion, but exhibit complex, multi-directional and, to some degree, unpredictable dynamics. Nevertheless, this model represents a useful analytical framework to visualize a "contingency approach"[7] to civil resistance and peacebuilding. This approach argues that complementary strategies might be applied sequentially or simultaneously at various stages of transformation of asymmetric conflicts, to initiate and support constructive change towards just peace.

## Figure 2: The progression of constructive conflict in unbalanced relationships (adapted from Curle 1971)

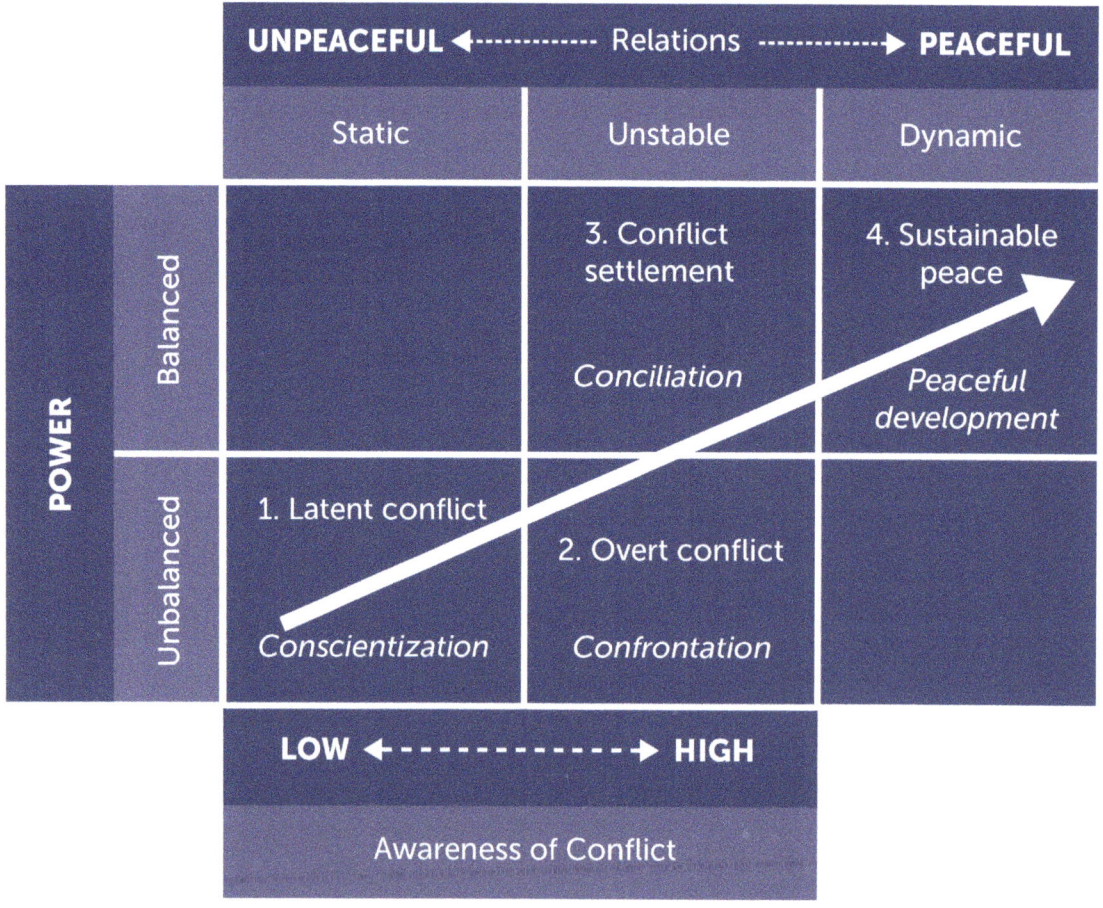

---

[7] The term is borrowed from Fisher and Keashly (1991), whose contingency approach to conflict intervention examines the complementarity and necessary coordination of third-party activities, and locates their failures in their inappropriate application with regard to the stages of conflict escalation and de-escalation.

## Stage 1 (Latent conflict): Conscientization through nonviolent mobilization

The initial stage in Curle's model, **latent conflict**, is characterized by a situation of structural violence that has not yet been expressed on the behavioral level. The relations between the parties are unbalanced and thus unpeaceful; they are also static, due to a lack of awareness of the situation of injustice or inequality on the part of the actors. In this stage, conflict transformation strategies need to awaken conflict parties to inherent structural contradictions that need to be addressed, while preventing such awakening from turning into violent mobilization.

Peacebuilding and civil resistance strategies place a strong emphasis on transforming "latent conflict" systems by resolving their root causes (such as political exclusion, socio-economic inequity, patronage and corruption, institutionalized racism, etc.) before they become manifested in attitudinal and behavioral violence. Peacebuilding practitioners are well aware of the importance of preventing violent conflicts by transforming unequal power structures. For instance, the 2015 Review of the U.N. Peacebuilding Architecture (adopted in 2016 as U.N. General Assembly Resolution 2282) emphasized the need for the U.N. to place much greater emphasis on the conflict prevention "toolbox." However, in practice, peacebuilders' conciliatory methods are ineffective at awakening and calling to action oppressed or discriminated groups in search of justice and empowerment.

By contrast, civil resistance methods such as community organizing offer potent "educational" (Curle 1971), "awakening" (Francis 2002) or "conscientization" (Freire 1972) means for the underdogs to develop their own political awareness of the need to address and restore equity, and to bring their acute collective grievances into the public realm. This is especially the case with nonviolent protest and persuasion methods (such as petitions, marches, or the displaying of cultural/political symbols). These methods offer mobilizing tools to increase consciousness and broaden participation in civil resistance campaigns. They do so by providing ways for all citizens to take responsibility for changing the situation (Clark 2005) and to disseminate public information about campaigners' overall goals and specific demands.

> ### Box 2: Conflict awakening in South Africa
>
> The founding document of the nonviolent liberation movement in South Africa, the Freedom Charter, served both as an awakening and mobilization tool. Some 50,000 volunteers were sent into townships and the countryside to collect "freedom demands" from the people of South Africa, synthesized into a final document adopted in June 1955 by 'Congress of the People.' It called for an end to racist white supremacy, establishment of democracy and protection of human rights, land reform, labor rights, etc. It inspired two generations of liberation activists who mobilized first through nonviolent struggle until the turn to violent insurgency in the early 1960s, and then again through a new wave of civil resistance by young militants in the 1980s (Maharaj 2008).

## Stage 2 (Overt conflict): Violence prevention through constructive confrontation

The second stage of Curle's diagram, **overt conflict**, is still characterized by power imbalance, but parties to the conflict have developed by now a high level of awareness of conflicting interests and needs. The tensions which were previously covered up (by the powerful) or met with apathy and resignation (by the powerless) have risen to the surface. The relations between the parties have become unstable, and the conflict manifested itself. For marginalized groups, this represents a stage of empowerment through (violent or nonviolent) confrontation—a term which Curle (1971: 176) employs "to cover all the techniques by means of which the weaker groups in unbalanced relationships attempt to change the character of those relationships, specifically to make them more balanced." While the subordinate group to an asymmetric conflict often perceives that the only effective strategy for pursuing justice is organized violence, such as guerrilla warfare, terrorism, or armed revolution, this report emphasizes that civil resistance offers a more effective and constructive approach to combating acute injustice and power imbalances associated with it.

Furthermore, peacebuilding strategies offer a wide range of techniques for societal groups to pursue peaceful change, but none of these may be characterized as "confrontation" tools. For instance, Paffenholz (2010) lists seven peacebuilding functions for civil society: protection, monitoring, advocacy, intra-group socialization, inter-group social cohesion, dialogue facilitation, and service delivery, but underplays the function of protest and resistance through which aggrieved groups seek to redress injustice and confront power-holders.

In the stage of overt conflict, civil resistance represents a necessary complement to peacebuilding, as it embodies the prosecution of necessary conflicts via unarmed, nonviolent means. The term nonviolent "struggle" used by scholars and activists alike highlights the "conflict intensification" dimension of civil resistance, by "making a hidden conflict more visible and open for purposive, nonviolent ends" (Fisher et al. 2000: 5).[8] Indeed, a certain degree of polarization between the adversaries is seen in "constructive conflicts" (Kriesberg and Dayton 2012) as a necessary step towards more peaceful relations in the future, facilitating their "ripening" for resolution. Writing from his prison cell in the Birmingham jail, Martin Luther King argued that civil resistance aims to "create a situation so crisis-packed that it will inevitably open the door to negotiation" (King 1964).

Civil resistance methods also contribute to peacebuilding by preventing the escalation of conflict prosecution into violent forms of confrontation. By acting both without violence and against violence, unarmed activists mitigate violence in both inwards and outwards directions (Vinthagen 2015: 12). Internally, nonviolent training programs and manuals (e.g., Popovic et al. 2007) stress the strategic importance of maintaining strict nonviolent discipline, and help campaigners develop "spoiler management" strategies to prevent and contain intra-movement violent flanks (Chenoweth and Schock 2016, Pinckney 2016). Civil resistance cannot prevent violent state repression against unarmed activists. Nevertheless, it is a self-limiting conflict strategy and a potential deterrent for mass atrocities. Nonviolent resistance is said to significantly reduce the likelihood of mass killings, in particular, because it is well-positioned to facilitate disobedience and defections among various allies of the regime, including security forces (Chenoweth and Perkoski 2015).

---

[8] The authors distinguish conflict intensification from "conflict escalation", whereby "levels of tension and violence are increasing" (Fischer et al. 2000: 5).

> ## Box 3: Genocide prevention through nonviolent resistance in Timor Leste
>
> The self-determination struggle in Timor Leste represents a successful example of a nonviolent resistance campaign against Indonesian occupation. It took precedence over guerrilla insurgency tactics and broke the cycle of violent escalation and brutal retaliation against unarmed civilians. Alongside the Armed Forces for the National Liberation of East Timor (FANTILIN), a Clandestine Front developed educational campaigns and nonviolent protests to raise awareness about the situation in Timor. The movement built momentum when massacres against unarmed protesters drew international outrage in 1991. Under pressure, Jakarta authorized a referendum in 1999, but reacted to the massive vote for independence by launching a scorched earth campaign that led to mass destruction and displacement. Thanks to the maturity of civil resistance leaders who called on FALANTIL guerrillas to remain inside their cantonments and to not resist with military force, the movement succeeded in de-escalating tension and preventing a civil war. Instead, an Australian-led international force was brought in and the Timorese were granted independence in May 2002 (Chenoweth and Stephan 2011).

Civil resistance should thus be seen as a necessary complement to institutionalized early warning efforts put in place by international or local organizations in conflict-prone environments. This also applies to recent efforts to "prevent violent extremism" (PVE): since there is a growing recognition that the "radicalization" of disenfranchised (Muslim) youths "is not necessarily the problem" and that the "[d]anger arises when radical movements start to use fear, violence and terrorist activities to achieve their ideological, political, economic or social aims" (UNDP 2016). Civil resistance might be seen as a constructive, self-limiting form of radicalism that addresses some of the same factors that tend to attract some people—particularly the young—to violent jihadi groups.

Civil resistance also seems to have a sustained, long-term impact on violence prevention: A seminal study demonstrated statistically that transitions precipitated by successful civil resistance campaigns "create much more durable and internally peaceful democracies than transitions provoked by violent insurgencies" since they are correlated with "a lower probability of relapse into civil war" (Chenoweth and Stephan 2011: 10; see also Karatnycky and Ackerman 2005, Bayer et al. 2016).

Finally, civil resistance methods have also been employed by communities in war-torn societies in opposition to all forms and sources of violence, including repressive violence by the state and insurgency violence by armed opposition groups. From peace communities in Colombia (Masullo 2015) to peace zones in the Philippines (Hancock and Mitchell 2007), such grassroots initiatives demonstrate that it is possible to engage effectively in organized nonviolent forms of noncooperation, self-organization and disruption even in the midst of armed conflict. Local war resistance campaigns contribute to peacebuilding by encouraging constructive engagement with conflict actors as well as prefiguring post-war peaceful societies, albeit on a smaller scale.

## Stage 3 (Conflict settlement): From resistance to dialogue

The third stage, **conflict settlement**, is reached once confrontation results in shifting power relations towards greater balance, leading the parties to reassess the costs of continuing stalemate (Zartman 1996). As the activists convert or coerce an increasing number of their opponents, the previously weaker party becomes a necessary partner in dialogue from the point of view of the pro-status quo party. The conflict thus enters a new phase whereby the adversaries resolve their incompatibilities with or without a third party, through conciliatory and problem-solving techniques such as negotiation, dialogue and mediation. Both peacebuilding and civil resistance strategies remain of a crucial importance at this stage, facilitating successful conflict settlement processes and outcomes.

### a) Civil resistance as a catalyst for more balanced and inclusive dialogue

Civil resistance can be considered as a pre-conciliation or pre-negotiation strategy because it accomplishes certain tasks necessary for an effective conflict settlement process (Dudouet 2013). In essence, through nonviolent empowerment, the underdogs increase their acceptability as a legitimate party in the conflict, and also their range of bargaining options. The gains made during the conflict are then legitimized at the negotiation table.

> **Box 4: Women's advocacy for peace in Liberia**
>
> In 2003 during the Second Liberian Civil War, a group of Liberian women from Muslim and Christian organizations, of both indigenous and elite Americo-Liberian classes, united to launch a nonviolent campaign for peace. The Women of Liberia Mass Action for Peace led mass protests against the fighting that swept the country at that time, urging Charles Taylor's government and the Liberians for Reconciliation and Democracy (LURD) rebels to cease violence and start negotiations. After forcing a meeting with President Taylor and extracting a promise from him to attend peace talks in Ghana, a delegation of Liberian women travelled to the negotiation site to continue to apply pressure on the warring factions during the peace process. They staged a sit-in outside of the Presidential Palace, blocking all the doors and windows and preventing anyone from leaving the peace talks without a resolution. Their actions brought about an agreement during the stalled peace talks. As a result, the women were able to achieve peace in Liberia after a 14-year civil war and later helped bring to power the country's first female head of state, Ellen Johnson Sirleaf (Gbowee and Mithers 2011).

*Through nonviolent enpowerment, the underdogs increase their acceptability as a legitimate party in the conflict, and also their range of bargaining options.*

By the end of the 1980s, the Polish Solidarity proved that the ruling communist regime, despite all its police and military power, was unable to defeat the national movement. Growing strikes and demonstrations put relentless pressure on the authorities, faced with a deepening economic crisis, to meet the demands of the movement. At the same time, through its strict nonviolent discipline, the movement became an acceptable interlocutor for the moderate communists. The legitimacy of Solidarity to govern Poland was confirmed during formal, round table negotiations with the regime that eventually paved the way for democratic elections that were won decisively by Solidarity in June 1989.

Civil resistance also helps to bring about more inclusive conflict settlement fora by empowering a civil society voice demanding participation in the design of post-conflict peacebuilding scenarios.

According to Curle (1971: 184-5), conflict settlement techniques such as dialogue and negotiation that are not preceded by power shifts towards greater equality at the bargaining table can result only in a pseudo-resolution, tantamount to prolonging the conflict. Indeed, a solution that does not guarantee the rights of the marginalized only reassures the top-dogs of their sense of power, while deceiving the underdog with some illusion of improvement of their situation. Therefore, the empowerment of the weaker party through civil resistance is a pre-condition for peacebuilding because it induces or forces the pro-status quo opponent to enter into dialogue about a solution to the conflict (Vinthagen 2015: 122), and it helps marginalized communities achieve sufficient leverage for an effective negotiation process (Finnegan and Hackley 2008, Wanis-St. John and Rosen 2017). Recent research on civil resistance provides statistical evidence for such claims by demonstrating the strategic superiority of nonviolent campaigns for democracy or self-determination in extracting concessions through bargaining in comparison with violent campaigns (Chenoweth and Stephan 2011, Pinckney 2014, Cunningham 2016).

---

**Box 5: People power and peace negotiations in Nepal**

The nonviolent revolution that shook Nepal in April 2006 achieved what 10 years of armed insurgency had failed to accomplish, namely, the negotiation of a comprehensive peace accord that democratized and stabilized the country. The combined peaceful mobilization of civil society activists, marginalized social groups and opposition parties through strikes, protests, boycotts and demonstrations, in alliance with Maoist insurgents who announced a unilateral ceasefire, had an immediate impact on violent conflict de-escalation. This mass-based movement (referred to in Nepal as Jana Andolan-II) incentivized foreign backers of the autocratic monarchy (such as Indian, U.S. and U.K. governments) to adopt pro-change attitude, and put pressure on King Gyanendra to reinstall the Parliament and to open a negotiation channel. This development eventually led to the signing of a peace deal abolishing the monarchy and establishing a democratic, secular and federal republic (Khatiwada 2015).

---

### b) Peacebuilding methods as necessary complements to transform polarized conflict scenarios

The "founding fathers" of civil resistance practice, exemplified by Gandhi and King, promoted a comprehensive approach to nonviolent conflict prosecution that would simultaneously fight injustice, resolve differences and bring about mutually satisfactory (i.e. win-win) solutions. Such approaches emphasize the need for nonviolent rules and techniques helping to break the spiral of destructive relations and offer reassurances to the opponents about their status in the post-conflict situation—thus laying the groundwork for inter-group reconciliation (Wehr 1979, King and Miller 2006, Vinthagen 2015). Most strategies and tactics employed by civil resistance activists are aimed at preventing conflict polarization and countering misperceptions, for instance by:

- emphasizing the distinction between people and problems or grievances ("hating the sin and not the sinner");
- seeking fraternization and reducing social distance with the opponents' pillars of power (security forces, business elites, religious authorities etc.); or
- maximizing inter-group contact and communication.

While building on these tactics and strategies, there is still considerable room to integrate conciliatory techniques that are part of the peacebuilding approach with the goal of ensuring more inclusive and effective change. In particular, in conflict characterized by a high degree of polarization over non-negotiable values such as identity or basic human needs, the transformation of power relations through nonviolent resistance does not automatically translate into positive change towards justice and reconciliation.

In this situation, dialogue is required to facilitate the articulation of legitimate needs and interests of all concerned into fair, practical, and mutually acceptable solutions (Lederach 1995: 14). Inclusive negotiations or national dialogue processes (Dudouet and Lundström 2016, Berghof Foundation 2017) are well suited to assist parties to identify key social structures that need to be reformed for equitable relations to come about. Confidential third-party assisted mediation can also provide an isolated setting to engage in quiet persuasion, where the powerful party may welcome an independent mediator as a means to change its policy without appearing to give in to public mobilization and pressure. These reflections highlight the need for in-depth comparative research on the "mechanisms of change" (Lakey 1987) that drive civil resistance-led transitions. Such research could seek to verify whether campaigns that are won through the opponent's persuasion and accommodation are indeed more conducive to long-term democratic outcome and civil peace than are more abrupt, coercive "regime changes" (Pinckney 2014).

> ### Box 6: Post-revolution transitions in Tunisia and Egypt
> While Egypt fell back to authoritarianism shortly after the 2011 nonviolent revolution, Tunisia is on a firm path to multi-party democratic consolidation. A major factor explaining these divergent post-civil resistance trajectories lies in the inclusive negotiation mechanisms put in place in the wake of the Jasmin Revolution which ousted the then President Zine el-Abidine Ben Ali, and at a time when social unrest threatened to escalate into civil war. In 2013, leaders of the successful civil resistance movement (a quartet formed by two major trade unions, the human rights league and the Tunisian Order of Lawyers) initiated a national dialogue that enabled a participatory process of decision-making on a pluralistic democratic 'roadmap' (Berghof Foundation 2017).

## Stage 4 (Sustainable peace): The twin roles of institutionalization and campaigning to promote and protect transformative peacebuilding

Conflict transformation reaches its final stage, sustainable peace in Curle's model, when the relations between the formerly conflicting parties become both peaceful and dynamic, as they establish and maintain healthy power relations. Democratization, reconciliation and development programs are introduced to encourage previously warring groups to rebuild their community and the fabric of torn relationships, and to prevent the conflict from relapsing into violence or instability at any time in the future.

Both peacebuilding and civil resistance approaches to conflict transformation are required to help post-war or post-struggle societies reach a genuine situation of positive peace, and ensure that the institutionalization of social movements does not ultimately result in their being co-opted by the state (Dudouet 2007).

### a) Institutional peacebuilding and the materialization of civil resistance gains

Thanks to its "constructive" dimension, civil resistance represents a creative form of conflict, in the sense that it prepares society for the post-settlement phase. Because it is strongly linked with social and political change from below and grassroots empowerment, it is often conducive to participatory democracy, which is also the purpose of peacebuilding activities in post-conflict zones (Francis 2002: 46). Collective nonviolent organizing in the form of constructive resistance actions provides invaluable experience in building parallel institutions, and honing skills of future democratic leaders who carry popular support. The emergence of future political leaders from civil resistance movements—such as Lech Walesa in Poland, Vaclav Havel in Czechoslovakia, or Aung San Suu Kyi in Burma/Myanmar—helps avert the external designation by third parties of spokespersons and negotiators who might lack grassroots legitimacy and popular respect. In this sense, civil resistance can be described as a "utopian enactment" of the desired future, by prefiguring a just and peaceful post-conflict society (Vinthagen 2015).

In turn, peacebuilding activities — especially Track I state-building processes — may help to maintain and institutionalize the creative practices and inclusive social experiments pioneered during civil resistance campaigns. Peacebuilders can incorporate the behavioral practices, normative principles and institutional templates derived from civil resistance into official peace infrastructures or legal codifications such as a reformed constitution.

### Box 7: Onset of democracy in South Africa

The institutions and mechanisms put in place in post-apartheid South Africa truly embodied and reflected the values and practices of the civil resistance movement that transformed the country during the 1980s (see Box 2). The 1996 Constitution embodied an inclusive vision of the social contract between state and citizens, introducing provisions for direct democracy and citizen participation in public policy implementation (Graham 2014). The 1996 Truth and Reconciliation Commission also became an international model for restorative justice. While it helped to reveal the self-limited nature of the African National Congress' armed insurgency and its scrupulous efforts to minimize civilian casualties (Maharaj 2008), some observers have argued that the TRC's memorialization efforts missed an important opportunity to raise collective awareness and pride in the legacy of past civil resistance struggles. Instead, the binary victim/perpetrator discourse and the sole focus on war crimes have obscured the heroic acts of nonviolent resistance against structural violence (Leebaw 2011).

### b) Civil resistance to "liberal" peacebuilding or incomplete conflict transformation

As noted earlier, the critical school of peacebuilding scholarship has shed light on the limits of post-war interventions by international superpowers that seek (intentionally or not) to replicate Western liberal democratic and economic standards. Recent studies have scrutinized local actors' various forms of subtle resistance to externally-led peacebuilding and state-building interventions, through the prism "everyday resistance." Some even noted its negative impact that "limits the smooth implementation of a measure intended to mitigate conflict or build peace" (Galvanek 2013: 16). Richmond (2010) coined the term "peacebuilding-as-resistance" in order to frame such uneasy interactions between local actors and externally managed peace interventions. Civil resistance scholars, however, view everyday resistance as something positive that can effectively shift the balance of power of particularly destitute, subaltern groups and help them survive and undermine repressive structures that can be supported by external forces (Vinthagen and Johansson 2013). The analytical lenses of civil resistance can help complement existing research on local opposition to ill-fitted peacebuilding programs by uncovering a wider range of individual and collective resistance methods at play.

> **Box 8: Civil resistance to externally imposed peacebuilding in Kosovo**
>
> Civil resistance against Serbian domination—combined with the armed struggle launched by the Kosovo Liberation Army (KLA)—played a pivotal role in raising international sympathy for the plight of Kosovo Albanians during the 1990s. Yet nonviolent tactics have also been mobilized in the post-war period, against a new opponent: international peacebuilding agencies. The movement Vetevendosje, founded in 2004, promotes popular resistance against the alleged structural violence exerted by the UN Mission in Kosovo (UNMIK), by imposing an externally driven local governance model deemed illegitimate and unaccountable to the Kosovar people (Ringler 2010). Asserting that the state-building project promoted by international peacekeepers stood in the way of Kosovo being able to become truly independent and sovereign, Vetevendosje activists have "combined popular protests, creative campaigns and local deliberations to propagate the right to self-determination, and to target the protracted and exclusive powers of the regime of international governance in Kosovo as the main obstruction towards achieving that goal" (Visoka 2011: 124-125).

This example illustrates the crucial function that civil resistance continues to play in post-war societies. The research community has paid little attention to nonviolent campaigns led by communities that have become disillusioned by the slow pace of reforms or abrupt returns to corrupt and undemocratic pre-settlement practices. Such mobilizations ought to play an essential role in ensuring that conflict settlements lead to sustainable peace as opposed to "pacification" merely "sweeping conflicts under the carpet" (Curle 1971: 184). By putting pressure on incumbent and new elites to follow on their commitments to comprehensive and transformative peacebuilding, civil resistance activists can arguably help prevent a relapse into violent conflict, by, among other means, mitigating the risk of accumulated grievances being hijacked by more radical, violent groups. In this context, it will be interesting to observe whether and how different civil society groups in Colombia mobilize to ensure that the commitments included in a recent peace deal between the government and the FARC are observed and implemented by all parties involved.

> ### Box 9: Post-war mobilization for positive peace in Nepal
>
> Despite the high hopes raised by the 2006 comprehensive peace accord in Nepal (see Box 4), top-down institutional peacebuilding mechanisms (such as the Constitutional provisions on ethnic federalism, the DDR programs or the Truth and Reconciliation Commission) have largely failed to deliver the promised 'peace dividends' to many sectors of Nepali society, who feel deeply frustrated by the government's failure to transform the deep-entrenched structures of exclusion and elite domination. Above all, this expectations-delivery gap affects historically marginalized communities from ethnic minorities, low castes and low-land regions. However, it also impacts other groups that have become marginalized as a result of the war, such as conflict victims or 'disqualified' ex-combatants. In the years following the peace accord, these various constituencies have mobilized through joint or parallel efforts in pursuit of their rights to truth, reparations, social justice, political representation, cultural recognition or economic wellbeing. While ethnic riots have grabbed the headlines, aggrieved groups have begun developing civil resistance campaigns, using a wide array of creative nonviolent techniques to create pressure on the authorities such as strikes and shutdowns (bandhas), painting over government signboards in the local (non-Nepali) language, organizing torch rallies, human chains and Gherao (encirclement of public buildings) (Neelakantan et al. 2016, Robbins and Bhandari 2016).

The final table on the next page summarizes the main features of the four conflict stages identified in Curle's model, the civil resistance and peacebuilding strategies appropriate for each stage, and their impact on conflict transformation.

## Table 2: Civil resistance and peacebuilding strategies and impacts during the four stages of conflict transformation

|  | Latent conflict | Overt conflict | Conflict settlement | Post-settlement |
|---|---|---|---|---|
| **Features of conflict phase** | Structural violence Low awareness of conflict Power imbalance | Conflict intensification | Conflict and resistance substituted by dialogue of equals | Peace implementation and consolidation |
| **Civil resistance strategies** | Community organizing/ mobilization Violence prevention | Nonviolent action (protest and persuasion, non-cooperation, disruptive and constructive resistance) | Popular pressure at the negotiation table for equitable bargaining outcomes | Nonviolent campaigns for full implementation of just peace |
| **Peacebuilding strategies** | Violence prevention (early warning, preventive diplomacy, dialogue) | Peacekeeping, dialogue facilitation (inter- and intra-party), human rights monitoring | Inter-party conciliation through (direct or mediated) dialogue and negotiation | Institutionalization of negotiation outcomes through political/security/ socio-economic reforms, reconciliation and transitional justice |
| **Impact** | Underdog's awakening to the need for conflict to address grievances and change the status-quo | Violence mitigation, empowerment of the underdog | Negotiated agreement | Sustainable peace with justice |

# Conclusion: Strategic contributions and takeaways for activists, practitioners, trainers, educators and international actors

Coming back to the initial questions put forward in the introduction, this report has sought to demonstrate that:

- Civil resistance and peacebuilding represent distinct strategies that share a common commitment to peaceful change and conflict transformation but prioritize diverse intervention tools. While civil resistance activists take a deliberate partial stance against perceived injustice and in favor of grassroots empowerment and nonviolent activism, peacebuilders seek to build bridges across conflict divides in order to restore constructive relationships and (re)build peace-conducive institutions. While civil resistance embodies contentious and extra-institutional methods of nonviolent conflict intensification, peacebuilding employs conventional methods of conflict mitigation. While nonviolent conflicts are waged through bottom-up people power, peacebuilding (in its most comprehensive form) is best supported by multi-track approaches to conflict intervention through coordinated efforts by international, state-based, civil society and grassroots bridge-builders.
- Only through the combined strengths of civil resistance and peacebuilding strategies can protracted conflicts rooted in structural asymmetry between state elites and their challengers (e.g., oppressed minorities or disempowered majorities) be effectively transformed. This report has analyzed the respective contributions of civil resistance and peacebuilding during the four main stages of transformation from latent to overt conflicts (through conscientization, mobilization, confrontation), and from peace settlement to consolidation processes (through dialogue, institutionalization, advocacy).
- Based on these complementarities, nonviolent activists and peacebuilding practitioners have much to learn and gain from each other, and international support ought to empower both types of change agents. For this to happen, the peacebuilding community needs to be better informed about the rationale

for, and potential contributions of, civil resistance strategies. Below are some initial reflections on possible concrete takeaways for these various constituencies.

## *Takeaways for grassroots civil resistance activists and peacebuilding practitioners*

- This report demonstrates the need for grassroots activists and bridge-builders to think more comparatively across the spectrum of conflict intervention strategies, and to root their choices of action in a thorough and ongoing analysis of power relations across conflict constellations. This would help them assess whether a given conflict might be "unripe" for resolution through negotiation or mediation approaches, and ought to be further intensified through constructive nonviolent resistance actions; and conversely, at which stage of a civil resistance campaign negotiation becomes possible and desirable.
- Curle's model as described here can be used as guidance by conflict stakeholders when confronted with the necessity to make crucial strategic choices, i.e. whether (and when) to escalate or to mitigate a conflict. But it may also be used by third-party advocates and mediators faced with the dilemma of whether (and when) to take an impartial stance or to side with the low-power/marginalized party to a given conflict.
- Further research is required to apply such a model combining civil resistance and peacebuilding strategies to the complex reality of contemporary conflicts. Although we know that highly polarized asymmetric conflicts require multiple forms of intervention, we still need to gain a more sophisticated understanding of the respective entry points for civil resistance and peacebuilding interventions in violent conflict.

## *Takeaways for civic organizations, trainers and educators that support and promote civil resistance*

- There is an acute need for innovative teaching and training material on the "new frontiers" of civil resistance, by applying its techniques and methods to the various stages of transitions from nonviolent conflict to peaceful and durable democracies. In particular, more in-depth knowledge is needed about effective mobilization tools during the crucial phase of post-war implementation of peace accords, which often gives rise to new grievances and frustrations due to both incumbent and emerging elites' inability or unwillingness to fulfill their commitments to inclusive reforms (Dudouet and Lundström 2016).

- Civil resistance teaching and training programs should also develop specific modules on the role of negotiation, dialogue and other peacebuilding mechanisms during, or following, nonviolent campaigns, including as skills and processes that may be used internally to build more effective coalitions and manage intra-movement conflicts; and seek to build partnerships with leading educational and practitioner organizations in the peacebuilding sector.

- Efforts must be made to collect case studies from around the world that illustrate how people mobilize nonviolently during different phases of conflict, for what purposes and to what effect.

### *Takeaways for international actors (donors, diplomats and inter-governmental agencies) seeking to identify, encourage, or support constructive and effective conflict transformation processes*

- The conflict prevention imperative has come to the fore on the international agenda thanks to recent U.N. global reviews on peacebuilding, peace operations and the fight against violent extremism.[9] Still, a mindset shift is required for peacebuilding agencies to embrace the language of "violence prevention," thereby recognizing that physical violence, rather than conflict, is the real problem. International intervention in crisis-affected regions tends to be driven by the imperative to avoid the overt manifestations of conflicts at all costs—including conflicts brought about by nonviolently mobilized populations. Such attitude might be ethically dangerous if it leads to the acceptance of highly inequitable relationships in the name of conflict prevention. In contrast, if they aim to address the root causes of protracted social conflicts, peacebuilding agencies

---

[9] See Review of the United Nations Peacebuilding Architecture: http://www.un.org/en/peacebuilding/review2015.shtml; Report of the U.N. High-level Independent Panel on Peace Operations: http://www.un.org/en/ga/search/view_doc.asp?symbol=A/70/95; U.N. Secretary General Plan of Action to Prevent Violent Extremism: https://www.un.org/en/ga/search/view_doc.asp?symbol=A/70/674

should be as concerned about unmasking structural violence and equalizing unequal relationships as they are about solving humanitarian crises or countering violent extremism.

• More concretely, there are some avenues that can be used to encourage international support for grassroots nonviolent activism for change. For instance, the globally embraced "Responsibility to Protect" imperative that encourages early action to prevent genocides and mass atrocities should also encompass a "responsibility to accompany" grassroots nonviolent movements rising in opposition to systematic violations of human rights (Lagon and McCormick 2015). Diplomats and other international actors already have at their disposable some guidance to help them decide why, when and how to lend their support to civil resistance movements for justice and democracy, and against corrupt state practices (e.g., Kinsman and Bassuener 2008, Dudouet and Clark 2009, Beyerle 2014).

• When preventive diplomacy fails to stop the escalation of violent warfare, peacebuilding agencies should be encouraged to identify, recognize and assist nonviolent flanks, which very often operate simultaneously with armed insurgent groups. Social movements that pursue similar goals to non-state armed groups while resisting the spiral of violence are often made invisible by the violent headlines of international media coverage. They often end up being sidelined by elites, armed groups and urban/professional civil society organizations alike when the time comes for participating in negotiations and subsequent peacebuilding mechanisms. If granted the prominence and recognition they deserve, such grassroots movements would have the potential to play highly constructive roles in post-conflict processes, thanks to their representative nature and democratic aspirations.

• More generally, and in line with the critiques addressed to liberal peacebuilding intervention in conflict-affected regions, it is high time for donor agencies, diplomats and supranational organizations to shift gears and move away from internationally driven efforts to restore or impose peaceful solutions to local conflicts. Instead, they should adopt a "light footprint" approach geared towards helping communities build their own capacities for constructive conflict transformation through the combined power of (civil) resistance and dialogue.

# Bibliography

Ackerman, Peter and Jack DuVall. *A Force More Powerful: A Century of Nonviolent Conflict*. New York: Palgrave, 2000.

Bayer, Markus, Felix S. Bethke, and Daniel Lambach. "The Democratic Dividend of Nonviolent Resistance". *Journal of Peace Research*, 53 (2016): 758–771.

Bartkowski, Maciej (ed). *Recovering Nonviolent History: Civil Resistance in Liberation Struggles*. Boulder: Lynne Rienner, 2013.

Berghof Foundation. *National Dialogue Handbook: a Guide for Practitioners*. Berlin: Berghof Foundation, 2017. www.berghof-foundation.org/fileadmin/redaktion/Publications/Other_Resources/NationalDialogue/BF-NationalDialogue-Handbook.pdf

Beyerle, Shaazka. *Curtailing Corruption: People Power for Accountability and Justice*. Boulder: Lynne Rienner, 2014.

Boege, Volker, Anne Brown, Kevin Clements, and Anna Nolan. "On Hybrid Political Orders and Emerging States: What is Failing – States in the Global South or Research and Politics in the West?". In *Building Peace in the Absence of States: Challenging the Discourse on State Failure*. Berghof Handbook Dialogue Series No. 8, eds. Martina Fischer and Beatrix Schmelzle. Berlin: Berghof Foundation, 2009. http://www.berghof-foundation.org/fileadmin/redaktion/Publications/Handbook/Dialogue_Chapters/dialogue8_boegeetal_lead.pdf

Boege, Volker. "Potential and Limits of Traditional Approaches in Peacebuilding". In *Advancing Conflict Transformation: Berghof Handbook for Conflict Transformation 2*, eds. Beatrix Austin, Martina Fischer, Hans J. Giessmann. Berlin: Berghof Foundation, 2011. www.berghof-foundation.org/fileadmin/redaktion/Publications/Handbook/Articles/boege_handbookII.pdf

Bond, Doug, J Craig Jenkins, Charles L Taylor and Kurt Schock. "Mapping mass political conflict and civil society". *Journal of Conflict Resolution* 41(4) (2016): 553–579.

Bond, Doug, Jenkins, J.C., Taylor, C.L. and Schock, Kurt (1997) "Mapping mass political conflict and civil society", *Journal of Conflict Resolution*, 41(4) (1997): 553–579.

Chabot, Sean and Stellan Vinthagen. "Decolonizing Civil Resistance". In *Mobilization: An International Quarterly* 20(4) (2015): 517-532.

Chandler, David. "The uncritical critique of 'liberal peace'". In *Review of International Studies* 36 (2010): 137-155.

Chenoweth, Erica and Maria J Stephan. *Why Civil Resistance Works: The Strategic Logic of Nonviolent Conflict*. New York, NY: Columbia University Press, 2011.

Chenoweth, Erica and Maria Stephan. How the world is proving Martin Luther King right about nonviolence, *Washington Post*, 18 January 2016. https://www.washingtonpost.com/news/monkey-cage/wp/2016/01/18/how-the-world-is-proving-mlk-right-about-nonviolence/

Chenoweth, Erica and Kurt Schock. "Do Contemporaneous Armed Challenges Affect the Outcomes of Mass Nonviolent Campaigns?" In *Mobilization: An International Quarterly* 20(4) (2015): 427-451.

Chenoweth, Erica and Evan Perkoski. "Government Crackdowns, Mass Killings, and the Trajectories of Violent and Nonviolent Uprisings". Presentation prepared for the 2015 Peace Science Society Annual Meeting. 2015. http://sites.psu.edu/pssi/wp-content/uploads/sites/12816/2015/11/Chenoweth.Perkoski.PSS_.pdf

Chupp, Mark. "When mediation is not enough". In *Conciliation Quarterly* 10(3) (1991): 12-13.

Clark, Howard. *Campaigning Power and Civil Courage: Bringing "People Power" Back into Conflict Transformation*. London: Committee for Conflict Transformation Support, 2005.

Cunningham, Kathleen. "Understanding strategic choice: The determinants of civil war and non-violent campaign in self-determination disputes". In *Journal of Peace Research* 50(3) (2013): 291-304.

Cunningham, Kathleen. "The Efficacy of Non-violence in Self-determination Disputes". Paper presented at the Annual Meeting of the International Studies Association, Atlanta, March 15 – 20, 2016.

Curle, Adam. *Making Peace*. London: Tavistock, 1971.

Dudouet, Véronique, "Peacemaking and Nonviolent Resistance. A Study of the Complementarity between Conflict Resolution Processes and Nonviolent Intervention, with Special Reference to the Case of Israel-Palestine." PhD Thesis. Bradford: Department of Peace Studies, University of Bradford, 2005.

Dudouet, Véronique. *Surviving the Peace? Challenges of War-to-Peace Transitions for Civil Society Organisations*. Berghof Report No. 16. Berlin: Berghof Foundation, 2007.

Dudouet, Véronique and Howard Clark. "Nonviolent Civic Action in Support of Human Rights and Democracy". Directorate-General for External Policies of the Union, EXPO/B/DROI/2008/69. Brussels: European Parliament, 2009. www.europarl.europa.eu/activities/committees/studies/download.do?language=en&file=25679

Dudouet, Véronique. "Nonviolent Resistance in Power Asymmetries". In Advancing Conflict Transformation. The Berghof Handbook II. Beatrix Austin, Martina Fischer and Hans J. Giessmann (eds.). Opladen – Farmington Hills: Barbara Budrich, 2011. 237-264.

Dudouet, Véronique. "Conflict Transformation through Nonviolent Resistance". In *Conflict Transformation: Essays on Methods of Nonviolence*. Tom Hastings, Emiko Noma and Rhea DuMont (eds.). Jefferson (NC): McFarland & Company Publishers, 2013. 9-33.

Dudouet, Véronique (ed.). Civil Resistance and Conflict Transformation: Transitions from Armed to Nonviolent Struggle. London: Routledge, 2014.

Dudouet, Véronique and Stina Lundström. *Post-war Political Settlements: From Participatory Transition Processes to Inclusive State-building and Governance*. Research Report. Berlin: Berghof Foundation, 2016. http://image.berghof-foundation.org/fileadmin/redaktion/Publications/Papers/IPS_SynthesisReport.pdf.

Fisher, Simon, Dekha Ibrahim Abdi, Jawed Ludin and Richard Smith. *Working with Conflict: Skills and Strategies for Action*. London: Zed Books, 2000.

Fisher, Simon and Lada Zimina. "Just Wasting our Time? Provocative Thoughts for Peacebuilders". In *Peacebuilding at a Crossroads? Dilemmas and Paths for Another Generation*. Handbook Dialogue No 7. Beatrix Schmelzle and Martina Fischer (eds). Berghof Foundation: Berlin, 2009. www.berghof-foundation.org/fileadmin/redaktion/Publications/Handbook/Dialogue_Chapters/dialogue7_fishzim_lead.pdf.

Finnegan, Amy C. and Susan G. Hackley. "Negotiation and Nonviolent Action: Interacting in the World of Conflict". Harvard Law School, 2008. www.pon.

harvard.edu/events/negotiation-and-nonviolent-action/negotiation-and-nonviolent-action-interacting-in-the-world-of-conflict/

Francis, Diana. *People, Peace and Power: Conflict Transformation in Action*. London: Pluto Press, 2002.

Francis, Diana. *From Pacification to Peacebuilding*. London: Pluto Press, 2010.

Freire, Paulo. *Pedagogy of the Oppressed*. Harmondsworth: Penguin Press, 1972.

Galtung, Johann. "Violence, Peace, and Peace Research". *Journal of Peace Research*, 6(3): 167-191 (1969).

Galtung, Johann. "Three Approaches to Peace: Peacekeeping, Peacemaking, and Peacebuilding". In *Peace, War and Defense: Essays in Peace Research*; Vol. 2. Copenhagen: Ejlers, 1976.

Galtung, Johann. *Peace by Peaceful Means: Peace and Conflict, Development and Civilisation*. London: Sage Publications, 1996.

Gbowee, Leymah and Carol Mithers. *Mighty be our Powers: How sisterhood, Prayer, and Sex Changed a Nation at War: A Memoir*. New York: Beast, 2011.

Hancock, Landon and Christopher Mitchell. *Zones of Peace*. Bloomfield: Kumarian Press, 2007.

Galvanek, Janel. "Translating Peacebuilding Rationalities into Practice: Local Agency and Everyday Resistance". Berlin: Berghof Foundation, 2013. www.berghof-foundation.org/fileadmin/redaktion/Publications/Papers/BF_CORE_Rep_Galvanek.pdf.

Graham, Paul. "Committed to Unity: South Africa's Adherence to Its 1994 Political Settlement". Inclusive Political Settlements Paper 6. Berlin: Berghof Foundation, 2014. www.berghof-foundation.org/fileadmin/redaktion/Publications/Other_Resources/IPS/6-South-Africa_s-Adherence-to-Its-1994-Political-Settlement.pdf.

The Guardian. "17 suggestions for supporting peacebuilding in fragile states". 21 July 2015. www.theguardian.com/global-development-professionals-network/2015/jul/21/17-suggestions-for-supporting-peacebuilding-in-fragile-states

Karatnycky, Adrian and Peter Ackerman. "How Freedom Is Won. From Civic Resistance to Durable Democracy". In *International Journal of Not-for-Profit Law* 7(3) (2005).

King, Martin Luther, Jr. "Letter from Birmingham Jail". in: *Why We Can't Wait*. New

York: Signet Books, 1964. 76-95.

King, Mary Elizabeth. *A Quiet Revolution. The First Palestinian Intifada and Nonviolent Resistance*. New York: Nation Books, 2007.

King, Mary E. and Christopher A. Miller. *Teaching Model: Nonviolent Transformation of Conflict*. Addis Ababa: University for Peace, 2006.

Kinsman, Jeremy and Bassuener, Kurt. *A Diplomat's Handbook for Democracy Development Support*. Third Edition. Waterloo (Canada): The Centre for International Governance Innovation, 2008.

Khatiwada, Padma Prasad. "The Nepalese Peace Process: Faster Changes, Slower Progress *Inclusive Political Settlements Paper 9*. Berlin: Berghof Foundation, 2014. www.berghof-foundation.org/fileadmin/redaktion/Publications/Other_Resources/IPS/The-Nepalese-Peace-Process.pdf.

Kriesberg, Louis and Bruce Dayton. *Constructive Conflicts: From Escalation to Resolution*. Fourth Edition. Lanham, MA: Rowman & Littlefield, 2012.

Lagon, Mark and McCormick, Patrick. "The Responsibility to Accompany: A Framework for Multilateral Support of Grassroots Nonviolent Resistance", *Ethics & International Affairs*, January 28, 2015. www.ethicsandinternationalaffairs.org/2015/the-responsibility-to-accompany-a-framework-for-multilateral-support-of-grassroots-nonviolent-resistance/

Lakey, George. *Powerful Peacemaking: A Strategy for a Living Revolution*. Philadelphia: New Society Publishers, 1987.

Lederach, John Paul. *Preparing For Peace: Conflict Transformation Across Cultures*. New York: Syracuse University Press, 1995.

Lederach, John Paul. *Building Peace: Sustainable Reconciliation in Divided Societies*. Washington, D.C.: United States Institute of Peace (USIP), 1997.

Leebaw, Bronwyn. *Judging State-Sponsored Violence, Imagining Political Change*. New York: Cambridge University Press, 2011.

Maharaj, Mac. "The ANC and South Africa's negotiated transition to democracy and peace". *Berghof Transitions Series 2*. Berlin: Berghof Foundation, 2008. www.berghof-foundation.org/fileadmin/redaktion/Publications/Papers/Transitions_Series/transitions_anc.pdf.

Mac Ginty, Roger. "Between Resistance and Compliance: Non-participation and the Liberal Peace". In *Journal of Intervention and Statebuilding*, 6 (2) (2012): 167-187.

Masullo, Juan. "The Power of Staying Put: Nonviolent Resistance Against Armed Groups in Colombia". *ICNC Monograph Series*. Washington DC: ICNC, 2015. www.nonviolent-conflict.org/wp-content/uploads/2015/12/ColombiaMonographForOnline.pdf.

Neelakantan, Anagha, Alexander Ramsbotham and Deepak Thapa. *Peace, Power and Inclusive change in Nepal*. London: Conciliation Resources, 2016. www.c-r.org/downloads/Peace,%20power%20and%20inclusive%20change%20in%20Nepal.pdf

Paffenholz, Thania. *Civil Society and Peacebuilding: A Critical Assessment*. Boulder: Lynne Rienner, 2010.

Pinckney, Jonathan 2014. "Winning Well: Civil Resistance Mechanisms of Success, Democracy, and Civil Peace". MA thesis. http://digitalcommons.du.edu/cgi/viewcontent.cgi?article=1516&context=etd

Pinckney, Jonathan. "Making or Breaking Nonviolent Discipline in Civil Resistance Movements". *ICNC Monograph Series*. Washington DC: ICNC, 2016. www.nonviolent-conflict.org/wp-content/uploads/2015/12/Pinckney-Monograph-Final-with-Map-Changes-for-Online.pdf

Popovic, Srdja, Slobodan Djinovic, Andrej Milivojevic, Hardy Merriman and Ivan Marovic. *CANVAS Core Curriculum: A Guide to Effective Nonviolent Struggle*. Belgrade: Centre for Applied Nonviolent Action and Strategies (CANVAS), 2007. https://global.wisc.edu/peace/readings/cambridge-canvas-core-curriculum.pdf.

Ramsbotham, Oliver, Hugh Miall and Tom Woodhouse. *Contemporary Conflict Resolution*. Third Edition. London: John Wiley & Sons, 2011.

Randle, Michael. *Civil Resistance*. London: Fontana Press, 1994.

Reichler, Luc and Thania Paffenholz. *Peacebuilding: A Field Guide*. Boulder, CO: Lynne Rienner Publishers, 2000.

Richmond, Oliver. "Resistance and the Post-Liberal Peace". In *Millennium: Journal of International Studies* 38(3) (2010): 665-692.

Ringler, Sarah. *The nonviolent resistance movement Vetevendosje in Kosovo: an analysis of conflict transformation and the promotion of social and political change*. MA dissertation. Berlin: Free University, 2010.

Robbins, Simon and Ram Bhandari. *Poverty, stigma and alienation: Reintegration challenges of ex-Maoist combatants in Nepal*. University of York, 2016. www.berghof-foundation.org/fileadmin/redaktion/Publications/Grantees_Partners/Final_Report_Ex-PLA_Nepal_May_2016.pdf

Rupert, James. "From Conflict in the Streets to Peace in the Society - How Can We Ally Traditional Peacebuilding with Non-Violent 'People Power?'". *USIP Seminar Report*. Washington DC: USIP, 2015. /www.usip.org/olivebranch/2015/08/05/conflict-in-the-streets-peace-in-the-society

Schirch, Lisa. *Little Book of Strategic Peacebuilding: A Vision And Framework For Peace With Justice*. Intercourse, PA: Good Books, 2004.

Schock, Kurt. *Unarmed Insurrections: People Power Movements in Nondemocracies*. Minneapolis: University of Minnesota Press, 2005.

Schock, Kurt. "The practice and study of civil resistance". In *Journal of Peace Research* 50(3) (2013): 277-290

Schock, Kurt. "Rightful Radical Resistance: Mass Mobilization and Land Struggles in India and Brazil". In *Mobilization: An International Quarterly* 20(4) (2015): 493-515.

Scott, James C. *Weapons of the Weak: Everyday Forms of Resistance*. New Haven and London: Yale University Press, 1985.

Sémelin, Jacques. *Unarmed Against Hitler: Civilian Resistance in Europe*, 1939-1943. Westport: Praeger, 1993.

Sharp, Gene. *The Politics of Nonviolent Action*. Boston: Porter Sargent, 1973.

Tarrow, Sidney. *Power in Movement: Social Movements, Collective Action and Politics*. Third Edition. New York and Cambridge: Cambridge University Press, 2011.

United Nations Development Program (UNDP). *Preventing Violent Extremism through Inclusive Development and the Promotion of Tolerance and Respect for Diversity*. A development response to addressing radicalization and violent extremism. 2016. www.data.unhcr.org/syrianrefugees/download.php?id=11412

Unger, Barbara, Stina Lundström, Katrin Planta and Beatrix Austin (eds.). "Peace Infrastructures Assessing Concept and Practice". *Berghof Handbook Dialogue Series* No. 10. Berlin: Berghof Foundation, 2013.

Van Tongeren, Paul Malin Brenk, Marte Hellema, and Juliette Verhoeven (eds.). *People Building Peace II: Successful Stories of Civil Society*. Boulder, CO: Lynne

Rienner Publishing, 2010.

Vinthagen, Stellan and Anna Johansson. "'Everyday Resistance': Exploration of a Concept and its Theories". In *Resistance Studies Magazine* 1 (1) (2013): 1-46. http://rsmag.nfshost.com/wp-content/uploads/Vinthagen-Johansson-2013-Everyday-resistance-Concept-Theory.pdf.

Vinthagen, Stellan. *The Sociology of Nonviolent Action*. London: Zed Books, 2015.

Visoka, Gezim. "International governance and local resistance in Kosovo: The thin line between ethical, emancipatory and exclusionary politics". In *Irish Studies in International Affairs*, Vol 22 (2011): 99-125.

Wanis-St. John, Anthony and Noah Rosen. "Negotiating Civil Resistance". *USIP Special Report*. Washington DC: USIP, forthcoming.

Weber, Thomas. "Gandhian Philosophy, Conflict Resolution Theory and Practical Approaches to Negotiation". In *Journal of Peace Research* 38(4) (2001): 493-513.

Wehr, Paul. *Conflict Regulation*. Boulder: Westview Press, 1979.

Wehr, Paul, Heidi Burgess and Guy Burgess (eds.). *Justice Without Violence*. Boulder: Lynne Rienner, 1994.

Woodhouse, Tom and John Paul Lederach. *Adam Curle: Radical Peacemaker*. London: Hawthorn Press, 2016.

Youngs, Richard. *From transformation to mediation: The Arab Spring reframed*. Washington DC: Carnegie Endowment for International Peace, 2014.

Zartman, I William (ed). *Elusive Peace: Negotiating an End to Civil Wars*. Washington, DC: Brookings Institute, 1996.